An Animal Family

OWLS AND OWLETS

By Gustavo Sandoval

Gareth Stevens
PUBLISHING

Please visit our website, www.garethstevens.com. For a free color catalog of all our high-quality books, call toll free 1-800-542-2595 or fax 1-877-542-2596.

Cataloging-in-Publication Data
Names: Sandoval, Gustavo.
Title: Owls and owlets / Gustavo Sandoval.
Description: New York : Gareth Stevens Publishing, 2018. | Series: An animal family | Includes index.
Identifiers: ISBN 9781482463859 (pbk.) | ISBN 9781482463873 (library bound) | ISBN 9781482463866 (6 pack)
Subjects: LCSH: Owls–Juvenile literature. | Owls–Infancy–Juvenile literature.
Classification: LCC QL696.S8 S75 2018 | DDC 598.9'7–dc23

First Edition

Published in 2018 by
Gareth Stevens Publishing
111 East 14th Street, Suite 349
New York, NY 10003

Editor: Ryan Nagelhout
Designer: Samantha DeMartin

Photo credits: Cover, p.1 rck_953/Shutterstock.com; p. 5 Vladimir Hodac/Shutterstock.com; p. 7 Palo_ok/Shutterstock.com; p. 9 Baranov E/Shutterstock.com; p. 11 Katho Menden/Shutterstock.com; p. 13 (top right) Stanislav Duben/Shutterstock.com; p. 13 (bottom left) Worraket/Shutterstock.com; p. 13 (bottom right) Ian Maton/Shutterstock.com; p. 13 (top left) dangdumrong/Shutterstock.com; p. 15 Dagmara Ksandrova/Shutterstock.com; p. 17 Nuwat Phansuwan/Shutterstock.com; pp. 19, 24 (owlet) bikeriderlondon/Shutterstock.com; pp. 21, 24 (nest) Anastasiya Rutkovskaya/Shutterstock.com; p. 23 CanadianTimber/Shutterstock.com.

Printed in the United States of America

CPSIA compliance information: Batch #CS17GS: For further information contact Gareth Stevens, New York, New York at 1-800-542-2595.

Contents

Owls are great birds!

They live in trees.

They have
very big eyes.
These help them see.

Owls have
big ears, too!

There are many different kinds.

Barn owls live many places. They have very strong beaks.

Baby owls are
called owlets.

They are very fuzzy.

Mother owls build a nest.
This keeps baby owls safe.

Mother owls look
for food at night.
They are nocturnal!

Words to Know

nest

owlet

Index